I Wish Sons Came with Instructions

I WISH SONS CAME WITH INSTRUCTIONS

Harry Rockefeller

ELM HILL

A Division of
HarperCollins Christian Publishing

www.elmhillbooks.com

Published in Nashville, Tennessee, by Elm Hill, an imprint of Thomas Nelson. Elm Hill and Thomas Nelson are registered trademarks of HarperCollins Christian Publishing, Inc.

Elm Hill titles may be purchased in bulk for educational, business, fund-raising, or sales promotional use. For information, please e-mail SpecialMarkets@ ThomasNelson.com.

Illustrations by T.J. Rockefeller

All Scripture quotations, unless otherwise indicated, are taken from the ESV° Bible (The Holy Bible, English Standard Version°). Copyright © 2001 by Crossway, a publishing ministry of Good News Publishers. Used by permission. All rights reserved.

Library of Congress Cataloging-in-Publication Data

Library of Congress Control Number: 2018951984

ISBN 978-1-595558329 (Paperback)
ISBN 978-1-595558725 (Hardbound)
ISBN 978-1-595558817 (eBook)

CONTENTS

FOREWORD

Why would someone write another book on raising sons? Isn't there already a plethora of them out there? You expect I would have anticipated that question, right? You can bet on that. I am hoping that through my storytelling of my real-life family events, you will get to know me: my likes, dislikes, motives, thoughts, as well as my actions. Well, now that for all practical purposes I'm done raising my three sons, I would like to tell my story—testimony—if you will. This is certainly not a comprehensive instruction book but rather an encouragement to go to *the* Instruction Book. Yes, indeed, children **do** come with instructions. If you have succumbed to the evolution worldview, then the answer is within the vast storehouses of man's wisdom. But if you believe, I mean really believe, the Bible, then just looking into that newborn's face you can see the Teacher-Creator-Redeemer image. Perhaps that was my first Holy-Spirit-inspired thought in raising my son. Instructions are in the Book written by our Teacher Creator Redeemer—the Triune God of the Bible.

INTRODUCTION

WHAM! The back screen door slammed shut. "Help!" I yelled. "Come quick! Jeffrey fell out of the tree. I think he's hurt. He was up really high in the tree."

My mom dropped what she was doing and as we both were hurrying toward the yard, she asked, "How high up in the tree was Jeffrey?"

I paused for a split second then answered, "Two Glennies high."

My 'yardstick' was the height of my older brother. "When I was a child, I spoke like a child, I thought like a child, I reasoned like a child. When I became a man, I gave up childish ways." I Cor. 13:11. Oh no, here comes my wife, Johnnie, piping in "I might disagree about you giving up several childish ways." OK. I must admit I am not God. I am an imperfect human. So, yes, the tales within these pages are mostly my "Godly" moments. I'll leave it to my wife to write the tome about my "Mr. Hyde" side.

Everyone begins thinking as a child: "How high in the tree was Jeffrey?" As we grow there are at least two more ways of thinking, speaking, and reasoning. One originates from the desire to please our Creator Redeemer God with a humble attitude grounded in the heart: a Biblical worldview. The other is some other competing worldview where 'self' reigns. As an example, consider the word 'success.' Quick, what thought just popped into your mind? If that image is one of wealth accumulation, it may reveal a materialistic selfish heart. If the thought is of some important person then this might reveal a heart focused on selfish pride or fame. On the other hand, Biblical success is defined in Joshua 1:8: "This book of the Law shall not depart from your mouth, but you shall meditate on it day and night, so that you may be careful to do according to all that is written in it. For then you will make your way prosperous, and then you will have good success." Johnnie and I attempted to model this pattern: speaking, thinking, and biblical reasoning in front of our sons. We sacrificed personal goals to accomplish the distant goal of raising boys into becoming men who hear and respond to God's voice. As promised, God has made our way prosperous in raising them. We still pray that our three sons will continue the process—becoming Biblically successful. Through it all I have been asked more than once, "How did you do it?" as if there were some rare script, or instruction book, on how to raise sons. The answer is both trivial and difficult. Trivial in the fact that, yes, it's just the Bible, but difficult in that it demands that I, the father, pick up my own cross—daily. Just as Christ was the example to show us the Heavenly Father, so too are earthly fathers to show Christ to their own sons. Oh, although Jeffrey was definitely shaken up, I don't remember him being seriously hurt.

Between my wife and me, we have held positions of baseball coach, soccer coach, soccer referee, royal ambassador counsellor, Sunday school teacher, children's worship music leader, not to mention those that come with the position: teacher, arbiter, and yes, Mom and Dad. It's been my experience that most boys don't get to grow up in a home with an earthly father who most often reflects his Heavenly Father. Many times the best a boy can hope for is an unselfish loving dad who willingly yields his own time, energy, and even personal goals to spend time with their son(s). My own dad was a man like that. However, I am convinced the Bible directs the man who is like that to press on in his "Biblical worldview." Philippians 3:14: "I press toward the mark for the prize for the high calling in Christ Jesus." How many fathers do you know who strive to teach a Biblical worldview to their son? How many men do you know who fit Joshua's description in Joshua 1:7—strong, courageous, who speak, meditate upon, and obey the Biblical Law book?

The preacher behind the pulpit said, "Let's have some testimonies since it's Father's Day." I had just graduated from high school and was daydreaming about going halfway across the country to a Christian college, Oral Roberts University, next fall. I have always been proud of the fact that I had committed to memory somewhere around 1,000 Bible verses. So, wanting to impress my girlfriend, I listened intently to what others were saying. I wanted to stand and say something grandiose about my own Father. One by one I heard great stories about—earthly—fathers. I began to feel a tug in a different direction. Not wanting to ignore my Heavenly Father, I stood and gave a testimony about Him. It wasn't that I didn't have anything good to say about my dad. In fact, I learned much about my Heavenly Father from him. Little did I know that come winter, my dad would be going back and forth seeing doctors about serious headaches. By the time his brain tumor was discovered it was too late. In March the next year, a week after emergency surgery and less than a year after that Father's Day, he died. After the funeral I travelled halfway across the country back to college. As a freshman in college I was reminded by the Holy Spirit: "I am a father to the fatherless." [Psalm 68:5 and many more.] If there is any good that can come from your good dad being suddenly taken when only eighteen years old, this was it. I had a promise that God Himself would be my Father, and I would never outlive Him.

Years later when the reality of my firstborn's conception sunk in, an overwhelming thought entered my mind. I would be responsible for raising my child for the next eighteen years or so. I became almost desperate for those how-to conversations with my dad. My next thought was a wish that this child-rearing process came with instructions. I then had a nonaudible but real conversation with the Holy Spirit. He reminded me the answers *are in the Bible*. I was responsible before God to "teach them diligently to my sons, talking about them when sitting at home traveling with them in the car as well as at bedtime and breakfast" [paraphrased, Deut. 6:7]; "I am to command my sons to obey God's Law" [Deut.32:46]; "I was to raise up my sons in the discipline and instruction of the Lord" [Eph. 6:4]. Then he asked me, *how willing are you to change yourself? If you want to influence your son to avoid your own mistakes in life, then you yourself must be willing to change.* Then He followed with *your example of being the father to your child is what your child will come to believe about their Heavenly Father.* "Train up a child in the way he should go." [Prov 22:6] I realized this was inevitable. If I avoided my son, he would learn to believe God was distant and unconcerned about him. If I spanked him out of rage, he would fear God as a tyrant. If I worked selflessly in raising him, then, he would believe that about God.

WHO IS IN CHARGE?

I said yes. I'll put myself under submission to God as my Father and ultimate sovereign over my family and me. I wanted my son to learn a Biblical (correct) image of God through my example. My wife and I began even before birth. We loved to sing to our sons even in the womb. One of our favorites, the classic song, "Jesus Loves Me," comes with profound words according to Karl Barth, a prominent theologian. For he has said that the most profound thought he ever had was "It was what my mother taught me in this little song. 'Jesus loves me this I know, for the Bible tells me so.'"

"ARGHHHHHHHHHHHH" my two-year-old screamed until his lungs were empty. Then again. I was awake by this time. Jumping out of bed, I took him into my arms.

"ARGHHHHHHHHHH."

He continued with his screams for a while. He was obviously frightened by something. Our conversation, if you could call it that, went back and forth, "What is it, Timothy?" then "AHHH," "Waaah," or heavy breathing. During this time I was planning my reasoned answer according to worldly wisdom. Then after "What scared you?" I finally made out one word, "monster," between his cries. Instead of my worldly-wise answer, i.e., to explain how monsters were not real, let's look under the bed and see together, etc.; the Holy Spirit stopped me cold. Instead I answered in the opposite by saying, "Yes, I know the monster was real." Suddenly, he stopped crying and looked straight into my eyes. His gaze spoke to me as if to say, *Finally, Daddy understands.* What was this tremendous revelation by the Holy Spirit that could cause me to make a 180-degree turn? He reminded me that in Romans 8:38–39 monsters are included in those things that are "never able to separate us from the love of God in Christ Jesus our Lord." I spoke to Timothy, "Jesus' love is stronger than the monster." Then I rocked him as I sang "Jesus Loves Me." He was sound asleep before the second verse. My sons began early to learn who I believed was in charge and about a chain of command. Many years later I had the opportunity to share this story in an interesting setting: "meet the teacher." I'll get back to that story later.

I am not educated in philosophy but looking back on this event, I realize now I had my first lesson in syncretism. Worldly wisdom, even in so-called Christian circles, would be the 'not real' response. However, biblical Christianity is clear: there is an unseen enemy. Both Old—e.g., powerful beings desiring to thwart God's will here on earth [Daniel 10:13]—and New—e.g. "We wrestle against … spiritual forces of evil in the heavenly places" [Eph. 6:12]—Testaments affirm this. The two different answers—monsters are real vs monsters are not real—result from two competing worldviews that don't mix, and in fact are opposites! In case you are still wondering what syncretism is, it is the attempt to fit, shoehorn if you will, an idea from one philosophical and/or religious system (worldview) into a differing worldview.

THE CHAIN OF COMMAND

The Bible explicitly teaches the family chain of command. The father is over his children and the husband is over the wife. As a helpmate in the home, the wife and mother holds her place between the father and children. I remember a childhood occasion when my dad let me and my brothers know that Mom was 100 percent in charge when he wasn't at home. I put that lesson to use. Whenever I found my wife needing to raise her voice or otherwise struggling with authority, I let my sons know I would surely punish them for an insurrection of that type. I followed through a few times. They quickly learned that Mom was not to be disobeyed or even talked back to. At the same time, I permitted my sons to hold any disagreement with me and promised that I would hear them out without them feeling angst. I wanted them to know they had my attention and both an open door to me by their submission to the one under my authority, their mom, who was the one they most interacted with. This reminds me of the Biblical pattern found in Hebrews 4:12–16. We have direct access to God the Father, Creator of the whole universe, because of our submission to the One he sent, Jesus, His Son.

"A ten-sh hut!" That drill sergeant in boot camp wants to be a pain. He acts as if he enjoys it when his authority is challenged, because in reality this chain of command grows stronger with "tension." By the time boot camp is done, the graduating recruit has learned well this military "family" structure. I recall causing a huge momentary disappointment to my sons that was encouraged by the Holy Spirit. I had taken my wife out on a weekend "date." Afterwards, with the whole family gathered around, we looked at pictures of our venture into a park because of a cave tour my wife and I enjoyed together. The park had one of the best playgrounds I had seen. I built up my sons' attention and excitement by talking about how big and high, oh, three or four times higher than I was tall, swings and slides were, making them sound ten times bigger than they really were. I also told them that both Mom and I talked about how much fun they would have had if they were there with us. Then, surprising my sons, I spoiled it all by saying I was glad they were not there with us. All three of my sons' faces dropped like a rock. Then I explained. I loved Mom so much that I wanted this to be a special time together with just her. They all were reminded they did not hold first place in Daddy's life. Their security of being in a loving home, where Mom and Dad's love for each other was unapologetically announced to be the most important, grew leaps and bounds that day. Our youngest son, T.J. (Timothy), caught that lesson. Now a young man, he knows the reason split parents buy frivolous gifts for their children. It's just an attempt to buy favoritism. This marital unfaithfulness magnifies insecurity in the children. Security, whether military or within the family, comes through experiencing faithfulness in the command chain above you.

1.1. House mouse poem [Prov 14:12; 16:2, 3, 25]

In 1986, when petroleum products were getting cheaper all the time, I found myself laid off from an oil company. The work I had been doing wasn't economical any longer. With three young sons five years old and less, our family suddenly found itself without steady predictable income. I was working on getting another job but it was taking much longer than I expected. I wasn't really losing patience with God but I admit it was a struggle. I wanted to depend upon God but also knew I needed to do some things too. About that time we had a mouse decide to come live in our home. I tried to catch it in one of those live traps, planning to let it go in the woods but that didn't work out. So I bought some standard mousetraps and set them. One night I awoke hearing a loud snap. Jeremy, my oldest son, heard it too. We both got up to see what happened. The mouse was trapped and obviously dead. It wasn't a pretty sight. My five-year-old Jeremy asked why that had to happen. I began to teach my son Proverbs 14:12 and 16:25 "There is a way that seems right to a man, but its end is the way to death." This also included teaching Isaiah 55:9 "For as the heavens are higher than the earth, so are my ways higher than your ways and my thoughts than your thoughts." We wrote a poem together.

> A small gray pretty mouse
> decided to make his home in our house.
> He stayed under our stove in the day
> but at night he came out to eat and to play.
> He didn't care to say please
> after he found that cheese.
> His thought was to eat what he could
> not caring if he should.
> That shiny metal post stood
> in the center of a shiny table of wood.
> The cheese was on this platter
> as if someone wanted him fatter.
> The humans usually left trash
> but he thought this was different; too easy? SMASH!

AUTHORITY AND RESPONSIBILITY

A chain of command obviously implies authority. But responsibility is always paired with authority. For example, many of our political battles between local vs federal control (authority) started out by voters relinquishing local and state responsibility to the federal government. Wait a minute, that's for another book; a different topic; back to raising sons. As I wrote earlier, both the Old [Deut. 32:46 and 47] and New [Eph. 6:4] Testaments clearly give parents responsibility and authority to teach their own children. After consideration of education choices, my wife and I decided to permit our sons to go to public schools. (Since then there have been school shootings and moral decay where "sexual orientation" of all kinds must be at least condoned if not embraced. Perhaps, were we to make that choice today, it would be different.) We both realized it was still our job to educate them and that began in an informal way much before the formal schooling began. Whether for the good or bad, I knew I was teaching, at least by example, the character (nature) of the Heavenly Father to my sons. But being human myself and not perfect, I sometimes had to swallow my pride and allow my children to educate me. I recall my middle son, Toby, telling me that it upset him when I raised my voice in disciplining him. Upon reflection of Scripture "Let your speech be simply 'yes' or 'no'; anything more than this comes from evil"

Matthew 5: 33–37. I realized he was right. I asked him to help hold me accountable for learning my lesson (not repeating the error). With everyone in the family including extended family of grandparents taking a role, learning was accomplished often before the subjects were introduced in public schools. I remember Toby coming home from school in second grade with a beaming face saying he actually learned something for the first time in school. As both their age and grade level increased, I took more interest in public school education—especially when the topic of sex education came up.

1.2. Dad and son, birds and bees day was special time

I wanted to be the one to break the news to my sons that their bodies would be changing in that growth time known as puberty. I planned a special day with Jeremy and several years later with T.J. where we played, rode bicycles, went swimming, and of course had the birds and bees talks. Toby reminds me to this day that he didn't get the special day. I found out too late his school was having their deal and so we rushed through the dad-son sex education talk in an evening at home. But I took each in turn (at the end of the special day) to see *The Man Who Ran*, a Christian open-air play, near one of our recreational lakes. The theme of the play was about Jonah trying to run from God instead of doing what God had called him to do. His calling on my life at that time was being a father to my sons. I desired them to not shy from their own general and special callings either. As the apostle Peter writes in I Peter 2:9, "A people for his own possession" with a job to do he warns the reader to "abstain from passions of the flesh" (verse 11) and goes on instructing about submission to lawful authority (vs 13–18).

1.3. Zygote probability [Matt 25:34; Eph 1:4, 5]

You can't avoid biology when the subject is the birds and the bees. Since I had done my undergraduate B.S. in Math and my senior paper topic was on 'probability,' I had to squeeze that in too. I began with something simple; something they could easily understand: flipping a coin. I could easily guess heads or tails. It's a 50/50 chance. But what about guessing the outcome twice, or more times in a row? I finally got to this astounding fact. Considering the probability of a specific egg from Mom and a specific sperm from Dad, the probability of my son being genetically who he is is equivalent to being able to guess correctly the Publisher's Clearing House 10-million-dollar winner out of the blue; not just once but twice in a row. I went through the calculations being sure they saw all those zeros. I reminded them that was how special and different from anyone else they really are. God had created each one on his heavenly "potter's wheel" unique, a one-of-a-kind. It's a blessing to understand our Creator God just a little in this fashion.

1.4. In grade school on parent day

Even as an older man, in many respects I'm still on that "potter's wheel." My Heavenly Father may interrupt me at any time. I need to always have a "will" that's soft to be reformed as needed on the wheel. It's always for my own good (Romans 8:28) and sometimes He interrupts me just to remind me He loves me. *How could I demonstrate that attribute of God to my sons?* I asked. *I'm limited. How could I butt in and remind my sons that I love them even when I wasn't there? How could I make my sons feel loved and special in unexpected spontaneous ways?* God answered my prayer and I'll share one example that I found fun. My sons, at least at the younger age, thought it was fun too. On "meet the teacher" day in the elementary grades, I would often be encouraged to sit at my son's desk. Getting bored, I would put love notes inside my son's books I would find there. Then during the year my son would be reminded at different times how much I love him.

1.5. Jeremy sixth grade - skills for adolescents

With my determination to obey my Heavenly Father, I took my authority and responsibility over my sons seriously. I had not always taken opportunities to "teach all things whatsoever Christ had commanded me" outside my own family. Over time as I grew older and wiser, I have found it less intimidating to speak about the role of Christ and the Holy Spirit to overcome "schemes of the

Devil" [Eph 6:12]. One of those times I was tempted to say 'no' or at least 'water it down just a bit', but didn't, was during a meet-the-teacher event in middle school. During the normal annual "meet the teacher," one class was left out. It was brand new. It also had the dubious title "Skills for Adolescents." I'm sure it was a required class so the schools could accept certain federal funds, but … didn't I drop that topic once already? Since the "Meet the Skills Teacher" was held later on a different day, very few parents, only about fifteen, made the effort to attend. Since there were so few, the skills teacher had us all sit in a circle. Then said the method she was holding the parent meeting would be exactly like the classes she had with my sixth grade son. Then she asked each of us to share something specific concerning the topic "Success in Communication with Our Child." Wow, another Holy-Spirit moment as three stories immediately came to mind of what I am sharing here. I truly felt in the center of my calling on that night when it came to be my turn to share. I could feel the tension and noticed some squeamish faces as I talked about Jesus and the Holy Spirit as real persons.

The clash of worldviews: biblical Christianity vs humanism was starting to become clearer to me. The very real sense that public education was evil became known in that event because what I shared would not be the content within the classroom where the public school teacher had responsibility over her sixth grade students, including my son. Even if the teacher believed what I said and wanted to share as I did, they wouldn't. It isn't allowed.

1.6. Jeremy eighth grade - viewing adult-themed films in public school

Two years later when Jeremy was in eighth grade, I received a letter informing me that the school was planning to show films about sex and sexually transmitted diseases. As parents we were invited to preview the films. So I did. I checked on my state law about what rights parents had and discussed the situation with my wife and son. After viewing the films, I replied with my own letter to the school official in charge. The public schools had "undressed" their worldview well enough for "sex education" that I couldn't help but notice the stark differences between what my son was being taught in public school vs. what his mom and I taught him based on the Bible. I got involved in school politics before general politics. I do have to agree that there are some good teachers but they are limited in what they can say or do. Humanism permeated public education and has the legal upper hand and not just in sex education.

1.7. I am a promise, I am a possibility

Occasionally, there are cracks in this humanistic culture. Our three boys filled one of those cracks when families were invited to present something at our elementary public school talent show. In fact, we have a video that I think one of our sons played at their wedding reception. Our three boys sang, "I am a promise" by Bill and Gloria Gaither up on stage in front of many other parents and school personnel. Their mom and I were in the audience beaming with pride—on second thought, I think I was occupied with the video camera.

1.8. Money

1.8.1 Rockefeller household budget
Secular humanism at its root places money and what money can buy as idols in place of God Himself. When I was laid off in

September 1986, I suspended my sons' allowances to help them learn the difference between "having a regular income" and "having all your needs met." I began to teach them the value and purpose of money and to let them know we were in this together. Over three months later Christmas came and I still didn't have another job, but we enjoyed our modest (cost anyway) gift exchanging. I can still remember those Christmas songs and events we shared as a family: putting up the tree and ornaments, etc. Not having money to spend as well as more time together made the family times that much more memorable and special. [Psalm 22; I Sam 30:3–6; Phil 4:19]. Weep with those who weep. Rejoice with those who rejoice. I think I shed more tears of joy that Christmas than ever before or since. With my job "allowance" cut off, I had to depend on my Father to meet my physical needs.

1.8.2. Actual budget

My wife and I attempted to put God's Law Book, the Bible, into action to come up with our family budget. It became obvious from Scripture that there were good reasons to do this. First, my Father as provider, protector, as well as savior, said to. In Malachi, chapter 3 verse 8 God says, "Will a man rob God? Yet you are robbing me. But you say, 'How have we robbed you?' In your tithes and contributions." Second, Jesus said, "Do not lay up for yourselves treasures on earth … for where your treasure is, there your heart will be also…. You cannot serve God and money."

Starting with these two main ideas, *we* arrived at six priorities. First, the number one priority is our tithe. We decided to give 10 percent of our gross income back to God, to our local church's general budget where we are members. The number two priority is necessities of life. Many identify this as "food, clothing, and shelter." To avoid having this either becomes a burden or an idol (the second main point above) in our lives, we made it a point to limit necessities of life to no more than 70 percent of our take-home pay. Our mortgage was our only debt and was included here. A few years ago, it was paid off but the same amount of money is still put away for property tax, home repairs, and home insurance. What is left over has been added to lower priorities, mostly priority four's "retirement." Besides utilities, necessary maintenance costs such as appliance and auto repair, gas for required travel such as commuting to work and our health, life, and auto insurance premiums are here. The third priority is a collection of other sub priorities: The top of the third priority at the time was our children's allowances they earned for doing chores. Just below that are "thank-you" offerings to God for meeting our family's financial needs. This includes offerings of benevolence and other special offerings to our church, donations to various health as well as Christian causes, etc. Next, I put maintenance costs of nonessential but very useful things such as our home internet service. The fourth priority are savings for real long-term items such as our sons' college costs, my own retirement, etc. The fifth priority—if there was any money left, that is—went to fixed optional costs. I started cable TV to watch the World Cup soccer tournament. I since have stopped cable TV. I buy magazine subscriptions unrelated to my profession. Other purchases in this category are: annual family vacations, birthday presents, soccer tournament fees, and trips. The sixth priority I call fun money. This would include "eating out," going to a movie, taking a long weekend vacation, etc.

I kept track of money spent by check book balance at the end of the month. I kept a minimum of $1,000 in our check book balance and then based on that permitted our family to spend priorities 3 through 6 accordingly the following month.

Priority	Percent of Income	
1	10	tithe
2	less than 70	food-clothing-shelter
3	2–5	thank-you offerings, useful stuff but not Necessity.
4	5–10	pay off debt, savings,
5	2	fixed optional things, family vacation
6	1	fun money

Certainly this detailed budget is not dictated by Scripture, but in practice does satisfy the two main Scriptural principles. I have heard God-focused arguments opposing such things as TV. Yes, I agree, my family would have been better off growing up without it.

1.8.3. 1,000 dollars at Christmas

I bought a used Ford Thunderbird for $1,300 before Jeremy, my oldest son, turned sixteen. I drove it a few times but it was not my primary car. It was soon to be his. He was doing well in school making good grades and playing club as well as school soccer. We made a deal that I would pay for the car, insurance, and gas. He would be financially responsible for only the maintenance. When he got his learner's permit, he started driving as most sixteen-year-old boys would: with abandon. I realized why his insurance was so much more than mine was, gulp. He ignored regular maintenance, would drive over curbs and other such nonsense. He paid for some of the repairs and maintenance but got behind, way behind, when we needed to put a new engine in the car due to his negligence. It reached a point where he owed Dad $1,000. Sure, he intended to pay up, but—really now? I had another conversation with the Holy

Spirit. What should I do? As usual, the Holy Spirit reminded me of my Heavenly Father's character through Scripture. Unless there is a miracle, money is a limited resource. God would not answer a selfish request for money with a miracle anyway. OK, I answered God, you want me to demonstrate Your (Heavenly Father) character by showing mercy; but I reminded Him that his two younger brothers were watching what I would do. This debt didn't happen in secret. God spoke to me of His character of Justice, or of treating all three of my sons equally. To emulate my Father, I needed to demonstrate both mercy and justice. Financially, this would cost me—and not just $1,000. The Holy Spirit reminded me of the cost to Heaven when Christ died for my sin in my place providing both mercy and justice. Christmas was coming and I desired to obey. When Christmas morning arrived, our sons each found an envelope with his name on it, sitting on our fireplace. The two younger sons opened their envelopes to find ten 100-dollar bills with a note from Dad, I love you. Jeremy opened his envelope and found an IOU note that said, "$1,000 paid in full," I love you. Dad.

1.8.9. Offer of PC at high school graduation

College is expensive. Costs are highly subsidized through scholarships, though. I looked at my possible financial future putting three sons through college and it wasn't pretty. I had been writing software to simulate aircraft behavior for a cockpit simulator manufacturing company. I had taken my sons there to see those simulators, letting them fly them. They caught my enthusiasm and I could tell they all were drooling for that newest fastest personal computer. So I offered a $3,000 computer as a high school graduation gift if they earned scholarships for college. Toby literally cut out pictures of $3,000 computers from the Sunday paper and worked hard. Jeremy, the oldest and first to go to college, earned a full-tuition scholarship. His brothers were both National Merit Scholars. And no, this probably was not the main incentive for them all to excel, but maybe it helped. Anyway, God financially blessed us all.

1.9. Feed your pet before you eat

Blessing, as well as "success", are not tied with finances. Going back to that Christmas when I didn't have a job was a different kind of blessing. I was blessed belonging to a loving caring family, including friends who brought meals over from time to time. But, with the new year—1987—coming, I can remember adding fasting to my prayers for my new vocation. My purpose for fasting is twofold. When I feel called or have a time-sensitive urgent prayer request, I know it is Scriptural and thus God-honoring. Also, my hunger is a reminder of the reason for the fast and a call (reminder) of my responsibility to meet with my Father through prayer. One of those things Christ taught us to pray was "give us this day our daily bread" [Mat. 6:11]. While on the subject of depending on God for our bread.... As children grow, they should be delegated responsibility. One of Jeremy's first chores was to feed our pet. Our family dog expected to be fed first thing in the morning. I taught Jeremy that his own hunger was a reminder that his pet needed food, and that feeding his dog came first. "If you want to be great in God's kingdom you need to be a good servant." [Mark 10:43] Hmm, what did Jeremy think about this? Maybe *What? A dog comes before me?* Often in servant leadership, meeting needs of those under our authority come before meeting our own needs. The mature knows we will receive our reward in the future. The immature are only concerned with *I want it now* or *What's in it for me?*

BUILDING CHARACTER

Perhaps the most quoted phrase said by those seeking the short-term gratification is "It's not fair." There's no telling how many times I've heard that from my sons. I usually responded with "Life's not fair." Even adults, myself included, find this lesson hard to accept. Before I go into the gospel story about this, I can recall many verses that teach us the perspective of "Life isn't fair." The main point is one of perspective. When we compare our self with another, without acknowledging God this is evil. David, in the Psalms, compared himself with others with one big difference: David knew God was his audience. He complained about the apparent success of the wicked to God. This is OK. Scripture teaches that many times God uses "Life isn't fair" experiences or feelings to draw our attention to Him. Toby was good in soccer. Early one soccer season, he broke bones in his foot when another player stepped on him, pushing him over. His season was over almost before it started. After we came back from the doctor visit, I felt drawn to go up and see him in his room. We talked about how life wasn't fair and how God sometimes uses that to give us course correction. He took this as a 'sign' to perhaps concentrate more on academics. Jesus told a story recorded in Matthew 20:1–16 about a vineyard owner who needed work done before dusk. He hired several at the start of the day working out business arrangements considered fair to both parties. Later during the day, it became necessary for the owner to hire more workers to be able to finish before dusk. Just an hour before sunset, the owner hired more to get the job done. At the end of the day he paid the last few hired first. Finally he paid those he hired early in the morning and gave them the same pay that he gave the first. The complaining started.

> And on receiving it they grumbled at the master of the house, saying, these last worked only one hour, and you have made them equal to us who have borne the burden of the day and the scorching heat. But he replied to one of them, friend, I am doing you no wrong. Did you not agree with me for a denarius? Take what belongs to you and go. I choose to give to this last worker as I give to you. Am I not allowed to do what I choose with what belongs to me? Or do you begrudge my generosity? So the last will be first, and the first last. [Matt 20:11–16]

2.1. Nickel for telling the pee-truth story

The flip (positive) side of "Life's not fair" is to have your self-esteem grounded in knowing the grace of God in Jesus Christ. Matthew 7:13–14 says, "Enter by the narrow gate. For the gate is wide and the way is easy that leads to destruction, and those who enter by it are many. For the gate is narrow and the way is hard that leads to life, and those who find it are few." Life is not fair because my life is one of the few that will not end in eternal destruction. Through faith I realize this Truth, by meditating on Scripture, especially the Psalms. My dad and mom were constantly teaching my siblings and me this Truth. My earliest memory of this truth lesson happened when I was only five or six years old. One morning my mom found our bathroom floor covered with urine. I don't know if she had the paddle in her hand but 'it' was certainly in her face

22

and voice. She summoned my brothers and me probably using our middle names too. "Who did this!" she shouted. My brothers spoke first, saying "Not I." Then my mom looked me in the face for my answer. Trembling, I admitted that it was probably me. I said I thought I remembered getting up to go pee but don't know anything else since I didn't remember anything. Her face melted. She called me aside and gave me a nickel (a lot of money at that time—ahh, inflation—another story for another time) for telling the truth. I've never forgotten that lesson. I looked for opportunities to show grace to my sons in similar ways.

2.2. Wisdom

As my sons were approaching those teen years, I realized peers as well as other interests pulled the attention of my sons away from me much of the time. However, there were teachable moments that I was able to capture and then use to my advantage. Also, as my sons grew older, adding wisdom to knowledge of the Bible stories became a priority. It's important to understand why the Bible stories are there. What was it that God wants us to learn from it? Here is one way I brought a familiar Bible story to life to my sons. King Solomon was known for his great wisdom. One day when I found my sons fighting over a dollar bill, I entered the fray and took possession of the dollar. I would be the judge and give it to the one whom I believed owned it. After hearing both sides, I still couldn't determine the proper owner. (I'm not nearly as wise as Solomon is.) Therefore, I tore it in half, giving each their 'share.' How many times have we seen children, whether young or old, fighting over something only

to end up with neither getting it? Both became losers. We followed that with the Bible story in I Kings 3:16–28 of the two mothers fighting over the one live baby. Solomon's decision to tear the baby in half giving half to each mother revealed the true mother.

2.3. Handling success

My sons were always excellent in academics and sports. We had a Tulsa-area track meet for boys in Royal Ambassadors, our church's boys-oriented organization. They came home with many track meet awards as well. I took this as an opportunity to teach my sons about the success of David, a renowned harpist, composer, author, poet, warrior, as well as handsome. He had everything in the natural to be proud of, but the Bible is clear about his strongest character trait: "David was a man after God's own heart." It's not wrong to burst with pride as long as the boast is in God. "David had success in all his undertakings, for the Lord was with him." [I Sam 18:14]. David also wrote "For this I will praise you, O Lord, among the nations, and sing to your name." [Psalm 18:49] The apostle Paul needed to discipline the Corinthian church. As their spiritual father, he had a responsibility and the authority to do this. Some questioned his authority. He told of many things he could boast in but summed it up this way in II Corinthians 12:9: "I will boast all the more gladly of my weaknesses, so that the power of Christ may rest upon me."

2.4. Persistence

Maybe your sons don't fit the description as one of those who are blessed with brains or brawn. Maybe you asked for help from God and you didn't get the answer or help you thought you needed at the time. With three young sons, we often had to all hop in our car and do things together. On one family Christmas shopping trip, the family split up so that Daddy (me) could go shopping for Mommy. Johnnie had Jeremy and our baby, T.J. I had Toby, at about three years old, tag along with me. He loved his independence, so I let him walk by himself as we entered a large department store. Inside I bought my wife a pair of green pants. Toby watched as the salesperson placed the pants in a gift box and then in a shopping bag. We were ready to go to the car, which was quite some distance away when Toby asked to carry the bag out of the store to the car. A serious but terse conversation followed: "No, the package is too big...." "But Daddy...." "No, you're too small...." "But Daddy...." "I said no...!" Tears started to flow. Then the God-idea hit me. If I carried Toby, then he could carry the green-pants package on his lap. I offered that as a suggestion and he gobbled it up, grinning from ear to ear. I still remember the two of us laughing our way out the store. "The eternal God is your dwelling place, and underneath are the everlasting arms." [Deut 33:27]. "They who wait for the Lord shall renew their strength; They shall mount up with wings like eagles; they shall run and not be weary; they shall walk and not faint." [Isaiah 40:31]. "And he took them in his arms and blessed them" [Mark 10:16]. "Cast all your care upon him for he cares for you." [I Peter 5:7].

2.5. Spank for disobedience only

The Bible is clear about the importance of discipline. In fact, corporal, or physical punishment is mentioned directly in Scripture. "He who spares the rod, spoils the child" [Proverbs 13:24]. But when, or for what offence, should a father or mother use the spanking board (rod)? Jeremy was finally big enough to do chin-ups on the fireplace mantle. The mantle ended up toppling over, spilling everything it had on it. One of those things was our Westminster Chime mantel clock and it broke. I got angry. In my flesh, I immediately wanted to place blame and the spanking board on my son. But I realized he probably didn't know the mantle was that insecure. So, since I had not instructed him that the mantle was not to be used for chin-ups, I held off the spanking. I made it clear the mantle was not to be touched. We got the clock repaired and the mantle never came down again.

LETTING GO

Quick Trip stores is one of the corporate sponsors of "Safe Place." "Safe Place" is a program to allow children to run away from home and seek shelter while a child-neglect or child-abuse is investigated. At times during spankings I've reminded my son that if they didn't like me running things my way, then all they would need to do was go down the street to Quick Trip. The irony was that we both experienced "comfort" after the spanking. Well, maybe I need to ask my sons that. The most well-known Psalm (23) in verse 4 says, "Your rod and your staff they comfort me." Today all three sons are married and on their own. Much like my own earthly father(hood) transferred suddenly to my Heavenly Father upon my own dad's early death, I can turn over the discipline part of fatherhood to Our Heavenly Father. He has more opportunity than I to continue this maturation process. At this stage in life, I also have confidence my sons will accept life's course corrections from God Himself.

The last stages of child and young-adult development involve the mind and will: cognitive reasoning. This stage of development may complete when the person is in their twenties or thirties, or unfortunately, maybe not at all. This is where the mind and desires come together around some perceived reality to mold a person's worldview that is then lived out. Most adults don't even think about that worldview behind, even dictating, their actions. Does your son know about syncretism: the attempt to reconcile opposing religious or philosophical belief systems? Does your son know the difference between "historical" Christianity and "progressive Statism" Christianity as defined by many evangelical groups? The famous Christian evangelical author, John Piper, recommends Christians stand down and not defend themselves with a gun. His argument is that he doesn't want to take the life of a perpetrator who, more than likely, is unsaved but who may, in the future, become saved. This was his response to Jerry Falwell Jr. whose argument is: we are to protect innocent potential victims, especially those we love; who encouraged concealed-carry on the Liberty University campus. Many Bible scholars overemphasize piety at the cost of not teaching a comprehensive biblical worldview. I heard a sermon about politics recently where the minister obviously mentioned Republican vs. Democrat but had nothing to say about the differences between their political platforms. I don't know if he is just scared of losing his tax-exempt status or if he really doesn't know how to handle or address those differences.

3.1. Discerning good from evil—eavesdropping

The Bible [Hebrews 5:14] says knowing the difference between good and evil is for the mature Christian. This is difficult to teach. In fact, the Bible says it comes by experience. Which "better good," or whose "rights," or what law book should be followed? Consider for a moment a court case somewhere in America. Personally, after hearing a tough case I would desire a judge to pray and fast (time permitting) to discern the legal truth. But alas, a judge here in the USA would be stripped of his authority if he did so. OK slap my face—this is for another book, another time. Is it good or evil for the NSA to snoop on everyone's email and phone conversations in order to stop a terrorist act? I caught my son eavesdropping on someone else's conversation in which he was clearly not invited to partic- ipate. I asked him to pray about whether or not that was good or evil. Daily I asked him if he remembered to pray and if he had his answer yet. Finally, on day four he admitted that it was wrong (evil).

Conclusion

Ephesians 6:4 wraps it up. "Fathers, do not provoke your children to anger, but bring them up in the discipline and instruction of the Lord." Sometimes fathers have asked me for pointers or help in raising their own children.

One time the conversation went something like this: "Your sons are so well behaved. How did you train them to be gentlemen?" My response was to explain how I taught them the Bible. For example, if their Sunday school lesson happened to be the David and Goliath story, I would say, "Great, let's read about it together." When I would get to the part about David carrying Goliath's head around the battlefield all day and then presenting it to Saul at the end of the battle, my son would say that wasn't in my lesson at church. Then I followed with, "Why would God think that it is important to put this detail in the Bible?" or "Why did David do that?" I would explain the hatred God has for sin and the awful consequences of sin. Sometimes I would remind them of the torture and death Christ suffered for them. I also taught my sons about how the Bible teaches capital punishment: stoning to death incorrigible children. In addition, I, as their father, would have to be the one to throw the first big rock. This particular parent didn't bother asking me for advice anymore. Maybe he thought I didn't love?

Our Heavenly Father is truly awesome. Think of His love, agape love. We can only realize how awesome agape love is in proportion to how far Christ was willing to go to pay our sin penalty. God truly hates sin. Both this agape love as well as true repentance and brokenness of our own sin borne out of fear fill the Bible's pages. This nature of God is eternal. For even in the New Testament, Paul in Romans chapter 8 talks of the one and only one who has the authority to make us "more than conquerors." This same Authority is the only one we need to fear. This is my yardstick, hopefully yours too. My success as a human father is in proportion to how much my sons picked up on both the closest I can come to agape love toward them as well as learning the fear of God—through me.

My favorite Bible passages

4.1. Micah 6:8

"He has showed you, o man, what is good, and what does the LORD require of you? To act justly, to love mercy and walk humbly with your God." For context, it is always good to ask, then what? Immediately in the next verse, we are reminded to fear God. Why? He can and does punish evildoers. Then the first evil act mentioned in verses 10 and 11 is about wicked treasure amassed with wicked weights and measures. Maybe God does have an opinion about whether fiat money is good or evil. Ahh, how many times now have I said that discussion is for another time or place?

4.2. Psalm 119:129–136

Many professionals have business cards. I have that too. I also have a "calling card," which gives personal information much like a business card but also gives information about my calling by God. The Scripture reference on my calling card is this.

Your testimonies are wonderful;
therefore my soul keeps them.
The unfolding of your words gives light;
it imparts understanding to the simple.
I open my mouth and pant
because I long for your commandments.
Turn to me and be gracious to me,
as is your way with those who love your name.
Keep steady my steps according to your promise,
and let no iniquity get dominion over me.
Redeem me from man's oppression,
that I may keep your precepts.
Make your face shine upon your servant,
and teach me your statutes.
My eyes shed streams of tears,
because people do not keep your law.

4.3. 2 Chron 7:14

"If my people who are called by my name will humble themselves and pray, seek my face, and turn from their wicked way, then I will hear from heaven, forgive their sin and heal their land." My wife and I pray this prayer often for our nation. We also add, "With God all things are possible" [Matt. 19:26].

4.4. Rev 5:12

"Saying in a loud voice, 'Worthy is the Lamb that was slain to receive all the power and riches and wisdom and might and honour and majesty and blessing!'" AMEN!

CPSIA information can be obtained
at www.ICGtesting.com
Printed in the USA
LVHW080028241118
598104LV00004B/9/P